Go To College For FREE

College Planning ABC's Guide To Finding Scholarships, Financial Aid, and Free Tuition Awards For College

MANUEL FABRIQUER

 భ STERLING PUBLISHING GROUP ಋ

CR SPG ∞

GO TO COLLEGE FOR FREE
College Planning ABC's Guide To Finding Scholarships, Financial Aid, and Free Tuition For College

Editor & Creative Director: Jodi Nicholson www.JodiNicholson.com

Cover Design by Jodi Nicholson for the Sterling Publishing Group, USA http://www.SterlingPublishingGroup.com

This book may be ordered through the publisher or by contacting the author directly at 408-918-3068 or at www.CollegePlanningABC.com

Published by
The Sterling Publishing Group, USA 813.720.7458
http://www.SterlingPublishingGroup.com

Printed in the United States of America
ISBN: 978-0-9884656-5-7

Education & Reference | Consumer Guides | College Planning
Business & Investing | Personal Finance | College & Educational Costs

DEDICATION

To my beautiful bride, Romina.

You are the love of my life,
and I thank you
for your love and support.

TABLE OF CONTENTS

INTRODUCTION

There are many resources on college, but there are not many resources or books that are available on the college planning process. This is the seed that fueled the creation of this book. It also helps that the college planning process is my specialty. I wanted to share some very important information about the whole college process, and make this a great guidebook for families with college bound kids.

There are three parts to the college planning process that I share with my clients: Admissions, Lowering the Expected Family Contribution, and Funding College. I organized this book in the same fashion and divided it into the same three sections so you can better understand the valuable components of each one.

A family will need to understand all aspects of this process in order to save the maximum amount of money for college and even go to college for free!

Although there are some resources in the marketplace today that discuss admissions and scholarships, I didn't find much data on the actual methods that truly cut down the cost of college along with the strategies on funding college. I also found information on creating college funds with 529 plans, UGMA/UTMA accounts, and prepaid tuition plans. These types of plans are techniques to save for college. Generally, these accounts are set up very early in your child's life so that you can gain significant amount of savings for college. However, if you have these types of accounts, this may hinder your family's ability to receive the maximum amount of free money for college.

This book will mainly focus on families who have children in high school and are approaching the college years. Most families who are in this category either have all of the money, some of the money, or none of the money for college. As you go through this book, I will be giving you proven strategies, and show you true case studies of families that I have worked with over the years. I helped these families to get into college with massive discounts, and some families were able to attend college for essentially, FREE!

Manuel Fabriquer, CCPS

Certified College Planning Specialist

http://CollegePlanningABC.com

PART ONE

ADMISSIONS

1. ACADEMIC PLANNING FOR HIGH SCHOOL

I wanted to keep the academic planning simple and focus on the general information. Many high school students must follow the basic courses to graduate. These courses are considered A-G courses. This is going to be the basic Math, Science, English, Social Science, and Art. In this chapter you will find an example of what students should be following in order to be admitted to most colleges. Note: I captured the information from the University of California website to demonstrate what criteria one would need to be qualified to the University of California system.

This is a standard at many colleges for admissions, yet keep in mind that taking approved high school courses *(listed as "A-G" in this section)* is not the only way to satisfy these requirements.

You also may meet them by completing college courses or earning certain scores on SAT®, Advanced Placement or International Baccalaureate exams.

General Standards For Admissions

First, lets look at the various categories, and then we'll examine the criteria and requirements for each.

- History / Social Science
- English
- Mathematics
- Laboratory Science
- Language other than English

A) History / Social Science

UC-approved high school courses

- Two years of history/social science, including: one year of world history, cultures and geography (may be a single yearlong course or two one-semester courses), and one year of U.S. history or one-half year of U.S. history and one-half year of civics or American government.

SAT® Subject Examination

- U.S. History: Score of 550 satisfies one year
- World History: Score of 540 satisfies one year

AP or IB Examination

- U.S. History: Score of 3, 4 or 5 on the AP U.S. History exam
- U.S. History: Score of 5, 6 or 7 on the IB History of the Americas HL exam.
- U.S. Government: Score of 3, 4 or 5 on the AP Exam satisfies a half-year.
- World History/Cultures/Geography: Score of 3, 4 or 5 on the AP exam in European History
- World History or Human Geography: Score of 5, 6 or 7 on the IB History HL or Geography HL exam.

College courses

- U.S. History/Civics/American Government: Grade of C or better in a transferable course of 3 or more semester (4 or more quarter) units in U.S. history, civics or American government.

- World History/Cultures/Geography: Grade of C or better in a transferable course of 3 or more semester (4 or more quarter) units in world history, cultures and geography.

B) English

UC-approved high school courses

- Four years of college-preparatory English that includes frequent writing—from brainstorming to final paper—as well as reading of classic and modern literature. Note, no more than one year of ESL-type courses can be used to meet this requirement.

SAT® Reasoning Examination—Writing section:

- Score of 560 satisfies first three years; score of 680 satisfies entire four-year requirement.
- ACT Plus Writing—Combined English/Writing: Score of 24 satisfies first three years; score of 30 satisfies entire requirement.
- SAT® Subject Examination—Literature: Score of 560 satisfies first three years.

AP or IB Examination

- Score of 3, 4 or 5 on the AP English Language and Composition or English Literature and Composition Exam.
- Score of 5, 6 or 7 on the IB HL English: Literature exam (formerly IB HL English A1).

College courses

- For each year required through the 11th grade, a grade of C or better in a course of 3 or more semester units (4 or more quarters) in English composition, literature (American or English) or foreign literature in translation.
- Courses used to satisfy the fourth year and/or the entire requirement must be transferable.
- For lower-division transfer, all courses must be transferable.
- Literature courses must include substantial work in composition.

C) Mathematics

UC-approved high school courses

- Three years (four years recommended) of college-preparatory mathematics that includes the topics covered in elementary and advanced algebra, and two-and-three-dimensional geometry.
- Approved integrated math courses may be used to fulfill part or this entire requirement, as may math courses taken in the seventh and eighth grades if the high school accepts them as equivalent to its own courses.

SAT® Subject Examination

- Mathematics 1C: Score of 570 satisfies entire requirement.
- Mathematics Level 2: Score of 480 satisfies entire requirement.

AP or IB Examination

- Score of 3, 4 or 5 on the AP Statistics Exam satisfies elementary and intermediate algebra.
- Score of 3, 4 or 5 on the AP Calculus AB or Calculus BC Exam satisfies three years.
- Score of 5, 6, or 7 on the IB Mathematics HL exam

College courses

- Grade of C or better in a transferable mathematics course that has intermediate algebra as a prerequisite satisfies the entire requirement. Freshman applicants cannot satisfy this requirement with statistics.
- Three semester units (four quarters) of non-transferable courses in elementary algebra, geometry, intermediate algebra or trigonometry, with a grade of C or better, satisfy one year of the math requirement.

D) Laboratory science

UC-approved high school courses

- Two years (three years recommended) of laboratory science providing fundamental knowledge in two of these three foundational subjects: biology, chemistry and physics. The final two years of an approved three-year integrated science program that provides rigorous coverage of at least two of the three foundational subjects may be used to fulfill this requirement.

SAT® Subject Examination—Each test clears one year:

- Biology: Score of 540
- Chemistry: Score of 530

- Physics: Score of 530

AP or IB Examination

- Score of 3, 4 or 5 on any two AP Exams in Biology, Chemistry, Physics B or Physics C, and Environmental Science
- Score of 5, 6 or 7 on any two IB HL exams in Biology, Chemistry or Physics

College courses

- For each year of the requirement, a grade of C or better in a transferable course in a natural science (physical or biological) with at least 30 hours of laboratory (not "demonstration").

E) Language other than English

UC-approved high school courses

- Two years, or equivalent to the 2nd level of high school instruction, of the same language other than English are required. (Three years, third level of high school instruction recommended).
- Courses should emphasize speaking and understanding, and include instruction in grammar, vocabulary, reading, composition and culture.
- American Sign Language and classical languages, such as Latin and Greek, are acceptable.
- Courses taken in the seventh and eighth grades may be used to fulfill part of (or all) of this requirement if the high school accepts them as equivalent to its own courses.

SAT® Subject Examination

The following scores satisfy the entire requirement:

- Chinese With Listening: 520
- French/French With Listening: 540
- German/German With Listening: 510
- Modern Hebrew: 470
- Italian: 520
- Japanese With Listening: 510
- Korean With Listening: 500
- Latin: 530
- Spanish/Spanish With Listening: 520

AP or IB Examination

- Score of 3, 4 or 5 on the AP Exam in Chinese Language and Culture, French Language and Culture, German Language and Culture, Italian Language and Culture, Japanese Language and Culture, Spanish Language, Spanish Language and Culture, Spanish Literature and Culture or Latin
- Score of 5, 6 or 7 on an IB Language A2 HL exam

College courses

- Grade of C or better in any transferable course(s) (excluding conversation) held by the college to be equivalent to two years of high school language. Many colleges list the prerequisites for their second course in language as "Language 1 at this college or two years of high school language." In this case, Language 1 clears both years of the requirement.

F) Visual and performing arts

UC-approved high school courses

- One yearlong course of visual and performing arts chosen from the following: dance, drama/theater, music or visual art

AP or IB Examination

- Score of 3, 4 or 5 on the AP History of Art, Studio Art or Music Theory Exam
- Score of 5, 6 or 7 on any one IB HL exam in Dance, Film, Music, Theatre Arts or Visual Arts

College courses

- Grade of C or better in any transferable course of 3 semester (4 quarter) units that clearly falls within one of four visual/performing arts disciplines: dance, drama/theater, music or visual art

G) College-preparatory elective

UC-approved high school courses

- One year (two semesters), in addition to those required in "A-F" above, chosen from the following areas: visual and performing arts (non-introductory level courses), history, social science, English, advanced mathematics, laboratory science and language other than English (a third year in the language used for the "E" requirement or two years of another language).

SAT® Subject Examination

- U.S. History: Score of 550
- World History: Score of 540

- Writing/English Compositions or Literature: Score of 560
- Mathematics Level 2: Score of 520
- Science (other than taken for "D" requirement): Same tests and scores as listed above under "D"
- Language Other Than English, third year
- Chinese With Listening: 570
- French/French With Listening: 590
- German/German With Listening: 570
- Modern Hebrew: 500
- Italian: 570
- Japanese With Listening: 570
- Korean With Listening: 550
- Latin: 580
- Spanish/Spanish With Listening: 570
- A second Language Other Than English: Same tests and scores as listed under "E"

AP or IB Examination

- Score of 3, 4 or 5 on any one AP Exam in Computer Science A, Computer Science AB, Microeconomics, Macroeconomics, Human Geography, Psychology, U.S. Government or Comparative Government
- Score of 5, 6 or 7 on any one IB HL exam in Economics, Philosophy, Psychology, Social and Cultural Anthropology, or Computer Science

College courses

- Grade of C or better in one transferable course beyond those listed above as clearing any of the "A-F" requirements; or
- A transferable course having as a prerequisite the equivalent of two high school years in a second language; or

- A transferable course equivalent to those that clear the "C, D or E" requirement; or a transferable course of 3 or more semester (4 or more quarter) units in history, social science, or visual or performing arts.

If you follow this standard of course work you should be in great shape for admissions to college.

You and Your GPA

Many students ask me, "What GPA is required to be admitted to college?" There is no real answer to this question, except to tell students to do your best, and work hard in school. The higher the GPA, the more opportunity you will have to be admitted to more colleges.

I want you to understand that there is going to be a college fit for every type of student. Everyone wants to attend the top universities in America—this is a fantastic goal to have—this illustrates that you are a very ambitious and driven person who believes in receiving an education from an elite college.

Admissions and Average Costs for College

Getting admitted to the top colleges in America is going to take some work. You are going to need more than just a good high school transcript. Colleges are going to consider your whole resume. They are going to review your extracurricular activities such as volunteer work, school participation, internships and/or work experience. It's going to be a combination of all of these things to be considered for admission into the Ivy Colleges.

What does college cost these days?

I'm going to give you some estimated figures that include housing, food, books and fees.

A public university is roughly $20,000-$25,000 a year. Since I'm in California, the college cost at the University of California level is about $32,000 a year. If you are looking at your private universities, you're definitely looking at $50,000-$60,000 a year. The elite private schools are going to run to you about $58,000-$62,000 per year.

It's a lot of money! Whatever college system you are considering to attend, I want to start off with a little bit of math.

Let's multiply the cost of the college that you are going to consider by four years.

Now let's multiply that by how many kids you have? Do you have your number?

Don't be surprised if it's a very large number—this could be a $300,000, $400,000 or even $500,000 cost to educate your kids.

This is a big number and very scary for many families. The typical age of parents that I work with are in their forties and fifties. Many are going to be facing retirement in the next ten to fifteen years. There have been some challenges in the past ten years with the economy due to stock market crashes in 2001, 2008-2009. The market since then has rallied, and some retirement accounts have "broken-even" or have a slight gain. The problem is the market is unpredictable, we don't know how well the stock market will perform in the next ten to fifteen years.

Let me ask you a few questions...

- Are you going to have enough money to retire?
- How is paying for college going to impact your retirement?

- If you pay for all of your child's college expenses, how much longer will you have to work?
- If you have all of the money for college, do you really want to spend it all on college?
- If you don't have enough money for college, how much debt are you going to have to consume to educate your kids?
- If you are going to take on debt to educate your kids, at what age are you going to pay off the debt?

My goal is to show you how to minimize that cost and how to take advantage of some strategies to lower the expenses of a college education. *If you can qualify for everything, your student may be able to go to college for* **FREE!**

I'm going to introduce strategies that could save you at least $40,000-$60,000 or even $100,000 off the cost of your college expense. Every family will have a different situation, and will have different opportunities to save money on college.

Regardless of your student's academic profile or your family income, there is going to be ways to apply for private scholarships.

I Can Relate!

Let me start off and tell you a little about myself. I'm a native of California and grew up in San Jose, CA. I come from a simple, modest family of six. My father was a laborer and worked at a local manufacturing firm in the bay area. My mother was a teacher by trade and worked as a Bank Loan Officer. We weren't rich by any means. My parents worked hard so that there was food on the table and a roof over our head. I learned very early in life of hard-work, honest-living, and integrity. My parents also taught me the importance of getting a good education and following my dreams.

And I did exactly just that! I earned my degree in Finance and Economics from the University of San Francisco in 1997. Since then, I have been pursuing my goal in reaching out and making a difference in the community. After college, I was a co-founder of a non-profit organization that helped with the youth in lower or single-income families. I found it very easy to connect with the kids because of similar roots. I understood the urgency to become a better person and not let my environment or situation dictate my future.

In 2007, this belief became my mission for my company, College Planning ABC. I have been helping students with their future by assisting their families properly plan for college. I have educated over five thousand families through my educational workshop events and seminars. I have helped thousands of clients that have invested in my college planning and consulting services either save a lot of money off the cost of college, or attend college for FREE.

I feel fortunate to have found my passion for helping students and families get through the college planning process. I find it rewarding to be a part of a family's life to help their student get into their dream college with minimum out-of-pocket expenses.

When I graduated from college I had a college loan debt of $60,000. With inflation, that amount today would be equivalent to approximately $150,000. If I had known what I know now, I could have gone to college for free! I was the ideal candidate for financial assistance. I was a good student with a 3.5 GPA, my parents did not make a ton of money, and I was one of four children to be the first to go off to college.

My parents said, "Hey, you know what, we would love to help you with college but we can't. We simply do not have the money. But, we will help you co-sign on loans."

That's definitely what they did—a whopping $60,000 worth of loans! I didn't know the process nor knew anyone to help me go through the process. I had no clue about any of it—the process, my financial aid options, available free money, and the list goes on. I knew nothing, nada, zilch! I simply entered the crazy maze of the college game, with no assistance in how to properly save, plan, or pay for college. And looking back now, I did a lot of things wrong.

Although, one great thing did happen to me when I was in college, I found and married the love of my life, Romina. She was actually my calculus tutor. I tell people, "You have to be pretty good to get your calculus tutor to marry you!" It's been 13 wonderful years being married to my best friend! We have been blessed with two awesome kids, Megan and Noah.

Which brings back me to the present day. I am here to help you avoid mistakes that can cause you hundreds of thousands of dollars. I am here to educate and guide you on the college planning process because, let's face it; the process is grueling and overwhelming.

It's a Maze Out There

It's a maze out there, and with no one to tell you what to do, how to do it, or when to do it, and so on, it's really complicated. When I was going through it as a teen, nobody told me how to fill out the paperwork, and nobody told me that it was going to be this complicated. I was lost, and as I shared earlier, I actually ended up paying way more money than I should have paid because I simply just didn't know the process!

When I was growing up, I wanted to be a super hero—I wanted to be a superman!

My mother always told me that I could do anything in life as long as I worked hard and believed in myself. She told me that if I wanted to be successful I would have to help a lot of people.

I want to be able to change people's lives in a positive way. I want to be able to make my footprint and impact the world.

When I was a little kid, I used to jump up and down on my parents' bed. I wore my little, bright red cape at the back of my neck, and I would think I could fly and someday, I would be able to save the world.

Today, I feel somewhat like a super hero. I go out every day and speak with parents and students about achieving their goals and dreams in life, and now I am sharing it with you in this book.

After college, I initially started my career in the financial world as a financial broker. In the financial industry, many of my clients asked me about how they would save for college, and/or pay for college. You may have the same questions.

What are the best ways to save and pay for college?

People were always asking me about buying real estate, holding it for ten to fifteen years and then selling it down the road to pay for college. They were investing in many different types of investment vehicles such as 529 plans, mutual funds, stocks, Coverdell accounts, UTMA accounts, and UGMA accounts to name a few.

Because there are a multitude of different vehicles to save for college, I decided to get educated on how colleges operate, and how they allocate financial aid so that I could best serve my clients.

I began my education on the college process. I learned how colleges have goals to admit students and how colleges allocate funding based on family need and student's merit. I discovered that college was really a business, and many families get lost in the crazy maze of the college process.

There is little or no support for a family to inform them about the pitfalls of the college system until it's too late. When I was in high school we went to the counselors, we went to the financial aid office, and admissions office, and found one thing. We found it to be really ridiculous— they did not help us! They didn't give us the information we needed to save money. They certainly did not give my parents peace of mind about my college expenses.

Why?

Because that's not what they do!

Later, I discovered that my parents were not alone. There are many parents who are terrified of how expensive it is today to provide their children with a college education. Some parents who are staying awake at night because they have no clue, and they need guidance. The parents need help to navigate through the dark tunnels of the college admissions and the financial aid system.

I asked myself, "Why don't I create a solution?"

So I did!

My whole goal with my company, College Planning ABC, my life's work, and with this book, is to help families live a happier, wealthier, and stress-free life; to effectively get through the college planning process with ease and peace of mind; and to be able to live their life without sacrificing too much from their lifestyle and their retirement.

2. TYPES OF TESTING

There are two different types of tests you need to understand: SAT® and ACT.

SAT® - The SAT® Reasoning Test (formerly Scholastic Aptitude Test and Scholastic Assessment Test) is a standardized test for college admissions in the United States. The SAT® is owned, published, and developed by the College Board, a non-profit organization in the United States and the nation's most widely used admissions exam among colleges and universities.

ACT - The ACT is a national college admissions examination that consists of subject area tests in: English, Mathematics, Reading and Science, and the ACT Plus Writing includes the four subjects plus a thirty minute writing test. All four-year colleges and universities in the United States accept ACT results.

A college will allow you to take either exam. However, you must take the writing section in each exam in order for the college to substitute scores.

Let's take a look at some general questions and information on testing.

What are the differences between the ACT and SAT®?

The ACT is an achievement test, and measures what a student has learned in school while the SAT® is more of an aptitude test that evaluates reasoning and verbal abilities.

The ACT has up to five components: English, Mathematics, Reading, Science, and an optional Writing Test, while the SAT® has three components: Critical Reasoning, Mathematics, and a required Writing Test.

In 2005 the College Board introduced a new version of the SAT® with a mandatory writing test. ACT continues to offer its well-established test, plus an optional writing test. A student only takes the ACT Writing Test if it is required by the college(s).

The SAT® has a correction for guessing which means they take off for wrong answers, while the ACT is scored based on the number of correct answers with no penalty for guessing.

Additionally, the ACT has an Interest Inventory that allows students to evaluate their interests in various career options.

How should I study?

Rent a book - Go to the library if you cannot afford to buy a book or attend a class. There is plenty of information that will allow you to study either on a CD, DVD, book, or kindle.

Buy a book - The book will cost you about $30 at the bookstore.

Buy a software or an online program - You can purchase a software at a bookstore or online for about $150-$495.

There are many online programs to consider. Take a look at the program at http://e-prep.com. If you like the program and want to save money on it, then contact my office at http://collegeplanningabc.com and we can assist you with getting a discount. We get this product at a wholesale rate and offer the savings on to our clients.

Take a class - Classes for SAT®/ACT varies and are based on the number of sessions and/or time spent with the students. Classes can range from $500-$3000. The average cost of a class is roughly $1500 for an eight-week course, or about thirty hours of classroom time with an instructor.

How do I send my scores?

You can use Collegeboard (http://Collegeboard.org) to send SAT® scores. You will be able to send your highest scores from all exams to the college. However, on the ACT, you will have to send the college all your scores.

How many times should I take the exam?

You could take these tests as many times as you wish. In my opinion, the third time is a charm; you may not get a much higher score after the third attempt.

And, you definitely want to study. I had a student that took the test six times to finally get the scores he needed to get into Loyola Marymount University in California. He took the SAT® three times without studying, and then he came to see me. I do not recommend this method—not studying for the SAT®. I do recommend studying well, and getting properly prepared.

So what happens if you take the exams and your student absolutely cannot score high enough to get into these colleges?

Every year, I have students with very high GPA's but low SAT®/ACT scores. If this is your student, you need to reconsider your college selections because it's going to be difficult to be admitted to the top colleges with low test scores.

What are other alternatives that you may need to consider?

Visit http://www.fairtest.org and view the list of approximately eight hundred colleges where your SAT® or ACT test scores are not weighed heavily in the admission process. They will look at your GPA, essays, activities, and/or what the student has done. They are going to consider other compensating factors that a student could contribute to their campus community.

How important are the standardized test scores?

The test scores vary between the large public colleges or private liberal colleges.

Large Public Colleges – Typically, GPA and the SAT® / ACT Scores are weighed 90% for admissions at many large state universities such as UCLA, UC Berkeley, UT Austin, and University of Washington. These are examples of colleges that heavily weigh the standard test scores.

Private Liberal Art Colleges – The test scores are weighed about 50% and the other 50% are the student attributes. This is because these colleges are looking for a different type of student; they're looking for students that are well rounded.

Colleges such as Reed College, Claremont McKenna, and Lehigh University are going to be very selective and will be looking for talented students with high scores and have a balance of academics and extracurricular activities.

3. FACTORS TO CONSIDER WHEN APPLYING TO COLLEGES

There are many factors to consider when you apply to a university. These factors will help you determine your ideal college.

Majors

Does the college that you are considering have a variety of majors or your major?

You may not believe this, but often students and parents will make a mistake on this very general criterion. Let me tell you a quick story about Chris. He comes to me and tells me that he wants to major in engineering. He also tells me that he found his number one college, and it's Cal Poly San Louis Obispo. Mind you, this school has one of the nation's leading Engineering Programs. He tells me that he has legacy and his grandfather, father, and brother all went to Cal Poly SLO. He said he's going to Cal Poly SLO.

I'm excited for him and I ask, "What engineering major are you going to consider?" He tells me, "Chemical Engineering."

I smile really big and tell him, "Give me a high five!"

Then I go on, "Guess what you get to do, Chris? You get

to pick a new school or a new major because Cal Poly SLO does not have Chemical Engineering!"

He says, "They don't?"

I reply, "No DUDE!"

Here's the lesson... Just because it's a good school or a legacy school, does not mean the college is going to have everything you want or need for your education and/or career choice.

Athletic Programs

Does your student want to play a sport?

Or participate in a club sport?

Maybe they want to attend a college that has a good sports program.

What about good sports teams?

A lot of kids watch ESPN and they say, "Hey, if I don't see that college on ESPN, then you know what, I'm not going to bother applying."

In the past five years, some colleges have raised a few eyebrows.

To name a few...Gonzaga University in Washington, OSU—Oregon State University, Fresno State University in California, and St. Mary's College in Moraga, California.

St. Mary's has been one of those colleges that have made the Sweet Sixteen or final rounds, or won championships.

Students are flocking to those colleges because they are now recognized as a brand name. People have heard of them on TV and think it's now a "cool school" to attend.

But there are a lot of great universities that nobody has

ever heard of because they're smaller liberal art colleges that are fantastic universities to attend. They do not have a large sports program and are not on national television.

Weather

Does weather have a factor in considering which college to attend?

Sure, many kids from California are interested in going to the east coast for college to experience areas such as Boston, New York City, or Chicago. I love these areas, and wow, what a great opportunity to be in a big city—away at college—where there are hundreds of thousands of college students from across the globe.

I tell students to visit these areas in the wintertime and then tell me how they like the cold. Most students in California have never experienced -15 degree weather. In California, we are spoiled. The coldest it may get in San Diego is about sixty degrees in the winter. Brrrr.

College Size and Number of Students

Some colleges have a student population of 3,000 and some up to 50,000. So which college is going to best fit your student? I don't know. Only you and your student can make that determination.

Do they want to be in a college environment where the average class is thirty students or the largest class is 500 students? Is that what you want? Is that going to be the best fit for your student?

Location

When I ask the mothers of their dream school for their student, the usual response is, "I just want to provide my son/daughter with a good education, as long as the school is within two hours driving distance—I need to see my baby!" Then I turn to the student, shaking their head, "I want to go out-of-state!" Location will definitely be a *driving* factor in determining your college list.

Financial Aid

Once you do get into that college of choice, let's say you get into that dream school, but they give you no financial aid, are you still going? If you get into Harvard, and there is no financial aid available for you, are you still willing to pay close to $60,000 a year?

How much do you value that high cost of education? Does it really mean that much to you? You should have a family discussion to see if that high-cost, dream school is still a consideration.

How do "students" pick colleges?

I meet hundreds of students every year, and this is one of the first things that I hear most...*"I'm so much in love."*

"Oh, my boyfriend..." or "It's my girlfriend..." and, "I'm in love. I'm so in love." And they go on and on. "We've got to be together in college. Oh, my goodness, Manny. We're so in love."

I laugh every time they tell me this because teenager's emotions at this stage are very intense, and they make emotional decisions.

Do you remember how it was to be young and in love?

I always tell students, "Hey, if it was meant to be, you'll be together forever. Go to college and do what's best for you, not what's best for your boyfriend or girlfrienod. "

Here's the next one: *"But, all of my friends..."*

"But all my friends are going there, and we've been going

to school together for the past ten years," or whatever it may be... "We've been together since the third grade, and we are **best** friends. We want to go to college together."

And I love this one ... *"It's a party school..."*

"It's a party school. Don't tell my daddy, all right?"

Well, there's a list of party schools that you could find online. If you go to the Princeton Review, search top party schools and you'll get a list of party schools in the nation that you can consider. You might say, "Hey, I didn't know that school is actually considered a party school."

Do you want to send your kid there?

Some colleges on the list may be well-known colleges that are highly regarded as being top in the nation. Is this news going to hinder your decision?

I tell families that every school is a party school, and if your student wants to go party—they will. There's a way to find a party to attend at any school.

Make sure you decide as a family on your college list. This will ensure that everyone is on the same page.

What do parents want in a college?

Now it's time to look at the parent perspective rather than the student. What do parents typically want, and what are you looking for in a university?

Let me ask Dad...

"Dad, what are you looking for in a college?"

Dad typically will say, "Manny, I want three things..."

"Money-Money-Money!" He continues, "I want the least expensive college out of my pocket, that's where we are going to go!"

Dad, I totally understand where you are coming from.

Let me ask Mom...

"Mom, what do you want in a college?"

"Manny, I just want a great quality education. I want my son or daughter to get the best quality education possible." Moms always give me that *look*, and sigh with a tilted head.

Maybe you went to school there

Tradition. Legacy. Alma Mater. Memories. Maybe you went to Carnegie Mellon, Rice, Reed, Claremont McKenna or NYU! Whatever college you went to, you loved the experience—you loved it there. You had a great time there and you want your kids to have that same experience.

Any School within two to three hours from home

"Any school, Manny, within two to three hours from home. Any school! Just find me the best college with a two to three hour radius from here and that is where we're going to go."

"Why?" I ask.

"Because if my baby gets hurt, or my baby gets sick, and if they need to go to a hospital, I need to get to them. I need to get to them, okay. My baby needs me..." Again, let me reemphasize, **location**.

Now, those examples are from real life clients. You may be chuckling, rolling your eyes, looking at your kid or co-parent and thinking to yourself, "Yes, that's you!" Here's what I want you to keep in mind and I want to pose it as a question: *"Does the college make the student, or does the student make the college?"*

Research and other factors

Allan Kruger, from Princeton University did a study with 1,500 students over fifteen years. He discovered the first job that the student gets out of college was based on the college that they attended. However, after five years of being in the industry, it really didn't matter anymore what college the student attended. At the end, it really is about the individual's performance and their ability to work with other people that determined pay increases and success.

Harvard Business Review wrote an article discussing promotions in the workforce. The article discussed that the reasons for promotional pay increases were based on a person's likeability, their ability to work in groups, leadership, and their ability to communicate with other people.

So, I ask you to consider what factors are most important?

4. WHAT DO COLLEGES WANT?

Let's talk about the key to admissions and answer the big question: **What do colleges want?**

Here's a quick checklist to make this easier.

- GPA
- Class Rank
- SAT® or ACT Scores*
- Extracurricular Activities
- Essay
- Special Skills or Talent
- Diversity or Residency
- Interviews (Note - not all colleges will have interviews)
- Recommendation Letters for private colleges

In this chapter I go into detail on the criteria for admissions but wanted you to have a handy list as a quick reference.

*Note - The colleges will be looking at your Critical Reading and Math scores for admissions. The writing portion will be considered, but it will be secondary.

Admissions Criteria

GPA - This is going to be the first thing that admissions will look at in your file. Each college will have different criteria for admissions. I want you to remember that there is always going to be a good college fit for the student somewhere. Remember, not everyone is meant for an Ivy League college or an alternative to Ivy colleges.

SAT®/ACT Scores - The colleges will take either exam. A conversion chart is made available to see how your score converts over. Visit http://convertyourscore.org/ and view your conversion scores.

Essay - Not all colleges require an essay for admissions. However, if they do require an essay such as UC Colleges or the Ivy League, then this is going to have an impact on your admissions. This is because most students who apply to the Top UC's or Ivy Colleges are excellent students with 3.85 to 4.0+ GPA's. The competition is very tough and the essay is going to be a way to distinguish the students apart. The colleges are looking for students that can communicate who they are outside of the classroom, and the essay should demonstrate growth, maturity, and reflection.

Extra-Curricular Activities - These are student's activities outside of their academics such as clubs, volunteer work, sports, music, work experience, and research projects. If you are applying to the Top UC's or Ivy Colleges this section of your application should be above the minimum requirement. For example, if you were considering UC Davis for a future career in Medicine, it would be beneficial to have volunteer or work experience in a hospital or research facility.

Special Skill or Talent - If your student has a talent in a certain area, you are going to want to highlight this information in your college application. For example: World Champion Irish Dancer, National Speech and Debate Champion. In addition, list the positions you held from a Team Captain of your Football or Debate Team to Leader of Youth Group.

Diversity or Residency - Colleges want a diverse student population; this does not necessarily mean a nationality, but it could also be residency. You may be Caucasian from California applying to a college in Nebraska or Oklahoma, the college may want you because there may not be many students from California applying to this college. Many colleges state that nationality is not considered in the admissions process, and it may not. Affirmative action has been removed from the admission process. However, colleges do want to have a diverse campus.

Interviews - Some colleges conduct interviews. However, interviews are not mandatory for admissions. The interview process can help the student or it can hurt the student slightly if the student cannot communicate or carry a conversation with the interviewer. Some believe that the interview will only weigh 5% of admissions. In my opinion, the TOP Colleges in America, the interview process is going to be very important and will have more weight on the application. I cover the interview process in greater detail in the chapter entitled: Why Have an Interview?

Recommendation Letters - Not all colleges require recommendation letters. Most students will ask for a recommendation letter from either their counselor or a teacher that they got an "A" in the class a year or two ago. The best approach to recommendation letters is for the student to request one in advance before admissions. Teachers and counselors will be writing letters for half, if not all, of the graduating class. It would be wise to get your request in early and set up a time to meet with the teacher or counselor to discuss your resume. The student should prepare a resume and discuss their activities and accomplishments. The student should also give emphasis to their personal development over the last three to four years. This is important so that the teacher or counselor can write substantial content about the student, preferably something outstanding.

5. WHY HAVE AN INTERVIEW?

An interview is your opportunity to show that you are more than just a stack of papers in the admissions office.

The goal is not to be a two dimensional candidate, but a multi-dimensional human being. If you are one of those special individuals endowed with a charismatic personality, the interview will be the ideal place to show your stuff, but even if you're the most introverted of students, be not afraid—this is not the end all, be all of your existence.

Interviews also give you a chance to relate how interested you are in the school. Since, through your research, you have an idea that the school may be a good fit for you, take the time to probe more deeply than what the sales literature provides.

Most interviews will be informational in nature. In these instances, the interview will be more about your questions concerning the school than the interviewer's attempt to evaluate you for placement in the college's freshman class. Did you understand that? It's about HOW YOU THINK and WHAT IS ON YOUR MIND rather than how you respond to the few questions that they're going to throw your way. In other words, go into the interview with a really positive attitude, as interviews usually just ENHANCE your chances with the university.

How the interview is conducted and by whom can tell you about the school as well. Is the interviewer a senior student employed part-time by the admissions office? Is he the person who will be reading your folder and who helps to make the admissions decisions? Is he an alumnus volunteering his time to help his alma mater?

Arranging for an Interview

Don't schedule your first interview at your top-choice school. In fact, most students should do a few "throw away" tours and interviews first. Practice makes perfect. You will do better after you have had some experience. Also, try to avoid making too many college visits or interviews in one day. Two visits is usually enough to overwhelm the senses. Schedule all interviews well in advance—like two weeks or more, if possible—and try to make them part of your campus tours. More competitive students will usually arrange for an interview with a department head, as well as the admissions person assigned to their region.

Preparing for the Interview

One of your goals should be to make a good impression, so be sincere and polite. Show the college that you know something about it and that you have something unique to offer. Be sure to read the school's catalog and preview their website, then write down a list of questions that you want to ask. Since the interviewer will have already reviewed your information, take time to think about your strengths and weaknesses, and be prepared to speak about them in a positive way. College interviews are not the time for modesty and one or two-word answers. Take stock of the extracurricular activities in which you have participated, along with your hobbies, volunteer work, and the other ways you spend your time. In other words, bring a copy of your transcript and activities resume to your interview. If there is something on your transcript that might need explaining, be prepared to properly address it.

Practice. Ask a family member or friend to interview you, or interview yourself in front of a mirror. Preparing in advance will make the experience more enjoyable for you because it will remove some of the anxiety of what to expect.

Mull over the sample questions provided in this chapter, and practice elaborating upon your answers. Think about the "whys" of the questions, and your reactions to them. Formulate your responses and practice saying them aloud to your family or friends. However, don't memorize responses. Clarify your thoughts about these subjects, but do not write a script.

In theory, you could be asked any legal question that bears upon an admissions decision. You might be asked any question, especially by alumni interviewers. It pays to be aware of the more common variations of obscure questions that come up from time to time. Again, don't try to script an answer and commit it to memory. Do be sure that you can handle the question in a relaxed, confident manner. Then, move on to one of the important points you want to make about your potential to contribute to campus life.

Now, here's a bunch of questions that admissions people may ask you:

Sample questions about your high school experience

What would your teachers say is your greatest strength and weakness both as an individual and as a student?

What would you say was your role within your high school community?

How would others describe your role in your high school community?

How would you describe your high school?

What courses did you enjoy the most?

Tell me something about your courses.

What courses have you enjoyed the most?

What courses have been most difficult for you?

What satisfaction have you had from your studies?

Has school been challenging?

What course has been most challenging?

What is the range of students at your school? Where do you fit in?

Do you like your teachers? What is your favorite teacher like?

If you could change one thing about your high school, what would it be?

What are the best and worst parts of your high school?

How do your classmates at your high school describe you?

Why did you pick the elective courses (or IB program or AP classes, etc.) you chose in high school?

Tell me about a milestone event that you encountered in high school.

Is there any outside circumstance that interfered with your academic performance? Tell me about it.

What has been your greatest experience in high school?

What is the most significant contribution you have made to your school?

Questions about your community

How would you describe your hometown?

What has been a controversial issue in your community?

What is your position on it (the issue)?

How has living in your community affected your outlook?

Questions about YOU

What is your strongest attribute? And your weakest?

What do you do in your spare time?

How did you spend last summer?

What do you do with any money you have earned?

Have you worked up to your potential?

Is your record an accurate gauge of your abilities and potential?

Why do you want to go to college?

What have you done to prepare for college?

What do you want to do in the future?

Tell me about yourself.

Tell me about your interests.

Tell me about your involvement in extracurricular activities.

Tell me about your family.

What is your favorite book?

Who is your favorite author?

Which of your accomplishments are you the most proud of?

What do you think about _____? *(Insert a current event or national headline from the past week.)*

If you could meet any important figure in the past or present, who would it be and what would you talk about?

If you could be any animal what would you be? Why?

Why are you applying to this college? *(If you've been there for a visit or tour, point that out.)*

What's your favorite subject?

What will you major in? Why?

What influenced your decision for this major?

How did you develop that interest?

What books have you read lately?

Of those books (or all books) what's your favorite? Why?

What extracurricular activity means the most to you?

What do you do for fun?

What specific skills will you bring to this college and to campus life here?

What do you plan to do after graduation?

Do you plan to go to graduate school?

Will you go right into _____ (career, profession, work) after graduation?

How do you describe yourself?

Where would you go if you don't get into this college?

Why do you want to go this region for college?

Has anyone in your family gone to this college?

Where do you see yourself five years after graduation?

What kind of career path do you see yourself taking?

Do you think you'll go to law school/med school/professional school? Why?

What extracurricular activity has been most satisfying to you?

What activities do you enjoy most outside the daily routine of school?

Do you have any hobbies or special interests?

Have you been a volunteer?

Would you make different choices of activities if you were to do it all over again?

What do you most enjoy doing for fun? For relaxation? For stimulation?

How do you spend a typical day after school?

What is of the most interest to you about our school?

What do you expect to be doing five years from now? Ten years?

Have you ever thought of not going to college? What would you do?

What critical world problem do you feel needs to be fixed, right now?

How do you view education?

Questions about your interests and activities

What personal traits would you like to see yourself build

in the next four years?

What articles and/or books have you read in the last year that have special meaning for you and why?

Do you have any hobbies or special interests?

In your life, what experiences have been most important to you?

Describe a challenge you've had and how you overcame it.

Questions about the college or college system

What questions do you have for the interviewer?

Why do you want to attend this college/university?

Why should we (the college) accept you for admission?

What is your career goal and how would a degree from this college help you achieve that goal?

What qualities make you a good choice to attend this college?

What other colleges are you considering?

What interests you the most about this school?

What's your impression of this college campus? (Include comparisons to your experiences on other campuses.)

Address how you feel about the social atmosphere or atmospherics at this college.

Are you aware that this college has an extensive core curriculum requirement?

Do you follow this college's sports? Which ones?

How do you feel about the campus culture?

How do you feel about our unique course requirements?

Who else do you know that went to this college?

Questions you may want to ask THEM

What are your concerns about the college environment/political stance/course work?

How does the student affairs division interrelate with the student body?

How effective is student government?

How is the college working to ensure students graduate?

Are there learning communities formed? How are they formed?

How involved are the professors with the students?

How do you judge student success?

Do you see significant grade inflation here?

After one year, what do the academic advisors cite as a major concern of the students?

Who advises students? How are they qualified?

How is discrimination handled on this campus?

How liberal or conservative are your faculty members?

How would you characterize student activism on your campus?

If you had one criticism of the students on this campus, what would it be?

Is "in loco parentis" alive or dead on this campus?

How would you rate the health care and health education of the student body?

How do your student affairs professionals handle increased parental involvement?

How has technology changed your campus in recent years?

How is your endowment fund spread amongst competing interests on campus?

How large are typical freshman courses?

How difficult is it to get into upper-level courses as a freshman?

I am considering majoring in _____.
How large are its freshman and upper class courses?

Is there opportunity for independent study or advanced research within most majors?

How does your university handle interdisciplinary studies?

What kinds of internship (or study abroad) experiences would be possible if I majored in _____?

How many students from last year's senior class went on to graduate?

Does this college give credit for courses taken on other campuses?

Does this college accept credit from only those campuses abroad where it has its own programs?

_____ is my first choice housing option.
What chance do I have getting it as a first-year?

How many upperclassmen live off campus?

How many students are typically housed per room? Are singles available?

How old are the dorms?

If there are fraternities or sororities on campus: How do

these organizations contribute to campus life?

I play _____. How actively could I become involved on your campus? At the intercollegiate level? In intramurals?

Is it possible for me to continue my (musical instrument) lessons on a private basis? Through your music department?

Off-campus, what cultural or recreational opportunities are available in the area?

What is the social and political atmosphere of the surrounding community?

How do students become involved in town life? Are there opportunities for service?

Can you characterize the personality or atmosphere of this college as you see it?

What kind of student is happy here? And what kind is not happy?

What kind of freshman orientation program is offered? How long is it and when does it occur? What activities take place?

How is the advising system set up for freshmen and who does the advising?

What are some of the best features of this college?

What are some of the challenges and even weaknesses of this college?

Are there opportunities for students to work on that?

How does the school treat AP scores? Is there a limit on the number of AP credits the school grants?

If the interviewer is an alumnus, ask him why he/she chose this alma mater over other schools.

What is the system for matching roommates?

How does advisement work?

What is the college's system for course selection?

Ask about your major. What new offerings are being considered? What majors on campus struggle to enroll students?

How is faculty turnover?

Are any new buildings planned? Why were those buildings chosen over other projects?

And here are some especially sensitive questions that you may (gently) pose to the college admissions personnel...

What is the profile of the type of student that gets "extra attention" in your admissions process?

Are there specific market segments that your university is trying hard to attract? Do you see that I fit into any of these profiles?

How is merit aid provided? Is it based on class rank, GPA, SAT®/ACT scores only? Or is there a "need" component to it?

How is your enrollment management system set up?

How many applicants do you wish to attract?

How many do you project to apply and matriculate?

What was last year's enrollment yield?

What is your college's discount rate?

For many colleges, your interest in them may be the most

important part of the interview. For them, the questions you ask indicate the degree of seriousness with which you're approaching the interviewer's college and the college decision generally. Therefore, the quality of thought you put into the questions you ask can be key. So, be thoughtful—avoid questions answered on the college's website. If your interviewer is an admissions officer, student or a recent graduate, focus on learning about the best professors and other academic resources, current events and the direction in which they see the campus moving. If your alumni interviewer is a graduate of more than ten years or so, get his/her judgments on how the college is evolving and how he/she and other alumni generally feel about the school. Within that framework, there are valuable things to know about many campuses. These interviews can be the best place to get thoughtful answers from someone who knows you, even a little.

Now that you've read through a snapshot of some of the questions that may come your way, and some that you may want to ask, let's look at a few general thoughts for approaching the interview itself.

Dressing for the interview

Women should consider nice slacks and a blouse, possibly worn with a blazer. A simple dress is also recommended. Shoes should be low to medium heels. Men should wear a minimum of nice trousers with a button down shirt. Let's not be pretentious, but also look respectable. Ties and suits are fine—if the environment calls for it. Consider these scenarios. What are the students in college wearing? Do you fit in this community? A turtleneck and sweater, or shirt and sweater are also possibilities. Jeans and caps can be fine too—if they convey who you are—but remember, you may run the risk of making an improper impression. Classic, conservative and simple is always a big hit!

Be aware of your body language

Everyone who has ever interviewed professionally will tell you that body language can tell a great deal about a person. Body language encompasses the physical cues that communicate information nonverbally, and interviewers are trained to pick up these signals. How can you send the right message with your body language?

Sit still and look directly at the interviewer. If there are multiple interviewers, look at the one who is asking the question at the time. Holding eye contact for more than five seconds at a time may be considered by some as intrusive. Others may interpret a person's lack of eye contact as a sign of being shifty or not trustworthy. Try four to five seconds of eye contact, then three to five seconds of looking slightly away, and then back again to making eye contact. Do not tap your fingers on the table or the chair arm. Do not tap your feet or swing your legs. Sit up straight in your chair with both feet on the floor. Breathing slowly and taking time to pause between your thoughts will help you stay calm.

The most important rule, however, is to be yourself and relax.

Personal Pointers

Know the time and location of the interview. Plan to be at least ten minutes early. Look at the campus map, where are you going to park? Figure this out beforehand, as time pressure can add ridiculous amounts of stress to this situation. When interviewing, speak positively about yourself without bragging. Be cheerful and friendly.

Remember that this is a professional setting; using colloquial language is inappropriate. Listen carefully to the questions you are being asked and answer them fully. Be wary of sensitive issues, such as religious or political affiliation. The interviewer may not agree with your viewpoints, so be respectful. Use common sense. Don't talk about how much you enjoy partying, dislike your physics teacher, or look forward to converting your future classmates to Druidism.

Saying "Thank You"

Campus visits take coordination, and that takes time and effort. The people doing the work are usually in the overburdened admissions department, which sets up arrangements for hundreds, sometimes thousands of students each year. Will sending a thank-you note make the difference between acceptance and rejection? Possibly, but that is not why you are writing the note. You are writing to thank people for making your interview and/or campus visit as comfortable and informative as they could.

Go knock it out of the park!

6. SELECTING A COLLEGE

How many colleges should my student apply?

In my professional opinion, I think students should have at least ten colleges. I like the number ten; it's a nice round number. Plus, I offer strategies in this section that create a good, solid mix of schools to profile.

What types of colleges should I have on my list?

You should consider three categories in your profile: **Reach Schools**, **Target Schools**, and **Safety Schools**. You should also have a good sample mix of public and private colleges on your list.

Let's take a closer look at each category.

Reach Schools - A student can possibly be admitted to Reach Schools, if your academic parameters are not within the school's range for the average incoming freshman. The probability of admission to these colleges is in the bottom 25%. With that said if you fall far below the required range, then it's going to be a REALLY BIG REACH, and you may want to reconsider another school. You may be spending too much time on the essays and application for a Reach School and the probability for your admission is very low.

Target Schools - A student can be readily admitted to

Target Schools, if your academic parameters are within (or even exceed) the school's range for the average incoming freshman. The probability of admission to these colleges is between 50% and 75%. I would not be surprised if you get admitted to several of your Target Schools.

Safety Schools - A student can also be readily admitted to Safety Schools, if your academic parameters fall far above the school's range for the average incoming freshman. The probability of admission to these colleges is greater than 75%. You should have better odds of being admitted to the university and most likely be considered into the honors program, or be considered for the higher amount of merit aid from the college. Most of the merit aid will be coming from the private universities versus the public colleges. The public colleges will give some merit aid, but it is highly unlikely they will give FREE rides. If you have a very high academic student with high SAT®/ACT test scores you will see scholarships that will allow you to attend the private college for the same cost as a public college.

Searching for colleges

There are many ways to search and determine if your student is going to be qualified for a college. Visit the website Collegeboard at http://www.collegboard.org to view college profiles, input your desired college profile, and see the range of admissions.

Some schools have software such as Naviance, and you can search the criteria and see the range of admissions for your college selections.

Another option is to go directly to the college's website and type "freshman student profile" in the search box on the site. You should be able to find the same type of information based on the prior year's admission class. When you find the information, you will see percentages based on 25%, 50%, and 75%. This will give you a good indication if your student qualifies for admission. If the student does not fall into the 25% of the incoming Freshman Class, I suggest that you consider finding another school.

I see many students and families picking colleges that are all reach schools. They apply to ten to twelve colleges that are all reach schools and the colleges have low acceptance rates. In these cases, the student's academic profile is average, and they are only applying to the top private or public schools. This is the main reason why having a good mix of Reach, Target, and Safety Schools is highly recommended.

Admission process

I'm an advocate for keeping things simple, just stay organized and stay on top of dates. You're going to have to stay on top of your admission deadline dates and your financial aid deadline dates. I recommend using a spreadsheet with the following headings for your columns, and updating it as necessary.

- College
- Admission Date
- Submission Date
- Essay Required (Y/N)
- Letter of Recommendation (Y/N)
- Subject Test Required (Y/N/Recommended)
- Sent Scores (Date)
- FAFSA Due Date
- CSS Profile Due Date
- Institutional Forms

- Notes/Comments

Why are admission deadlines all different?

This can be confusing because you will notice that colleges have different admission dates based on *Early Decision*, *Early Action*, and *Regular Decision*.

Early Decision - This is a binding agreement with the college, and if admitted your student will have to attend. You will be notified within 3-6 weeks, typically by the end of December of the admission decision. The rule of thumb is that if you apply for Early Decision, there may not be much financial aid. Some colleges state that there is no financial impact on financial aid, and *that* they admit blindly.

In my opinion, there are colleges that hold this true, while other colleges do look at your finances. If you are going to consider going Early Decision, just make sure you are willing to pay the price of the college if they are not going to give you enough free money. Let me give you a family case study, the personal information has been altered; however results depict actual data.

Jason: 3.6 GPA, SAT® scores 2030

Applied to Reed College Early Decision: Accepted

Family Income: $180,000 with 3 children; 1 student in college, plus Jason entering college

Renting: No home equity

Assets: 529 plan $35,000

Stocks and Cash: $80,000

EFC with 2 kids in college $24,700 Federal, and $ 25,701 Institutional EFC

Cost of Attendance: $62,000

Based on EFC they should receive at least $25,000-$30,000 of need based aid, yet they did not.

An important factor in this case is that Reed College is a need-based college, and does not give any merit-based awards. This is why we applied to this college, for the need-based aid; yet the only aid received was a $7000 grant, work-study of $3000, and a $5,500 student loan.

We did the appeal and the family was informed that the early application pool was very competitive and that they cannot give any more money.

Here is what was considered: The student came into the college in the lower part of the admissions pool. The family had a $35,000 529 plan that must be used for college. This student was not really competitive with the incoming freshman class, and Reed reviewed the other colleges that the student applied to and knew that this family wanted Jason to attend Reed College. Since he applied Early Decision and because he was in the lower bracket of the incoming freshman class, he received very little money to attend Reed.

My point is that if you commit to Early Decision and your student is not at the top of the admission chart, you may have difficulty getting any type of need or merit based awards. You will increase your odds of admission by applying Early Decision, but I prefer the college with FREE money.

If you apply for Early Decision just make sure you are willing to pay a larger portion for college than what you may initially intend. Early Decision is for those families who really want to attend a certain college and are willing to pay full price, any discounts will be a bonus.

Early Action - This is a non-binding agreement with the college and your student will have until May 1st to consider admissions.

Regular Decision - If you are going to apply for regular decision, please take a look at the college's website for the dates. The deadlines vary and can be in November-March. It will depend on the college that you are considering.

It is important to let your high school counselor know your deadline dates for admissions so that they can send your transcripts to the college.

The student is responsible for sending out the SAT®/ACT test scores to the colleges on time. It may take a few weeks for the scores to arrive, so make sure that it's done with ample time.

Remember, use a spreadsheet and keep track of your action steps for admission.

How am I supposed to pay for college?

I cover this is detail in the section on FUNDING, yet I wanted to begin the discussion here as part of the selection process.

College expenses are typically the cost of attendance with room and board.

If you are planning to attend an out-of-state State college, there may be a higher fee. If you are in California, there is an exchange program called the Western Undergraduate Exchange. This will allow you to attend a college out-of-state for a discounted rate. You must first understand the criteria for obtaining the discount. Some colleges may be on the list, however if the major that you are considering is not on the list, you may not be eligible for the discounted pricing.

I also want you to consider the graduation rates at the college. The National Center for Educational Statistics states that 60.8 percent of all public university student graduate in about six years. Ouch!

When calculating how much money you need to spend for college, you need to add on two more years for each student if you are going to a public university. In many public colleges, departments are impacted and students find it difficult to graduate in four years. The goal is really to get your student done in four years, not five and a half to six years.

Currently in California, there are budget cuts and these cuts are impacting the amount of classes available and enrollment. Classes fill up fast! I'm not saying that your student cannot graduate in four years if they attend a public college—they may have to work a little harder. Students can take summer school to complete some of the general education requirements, and they may take 18-21 units a semester.

In my opinion, the longer a student has to stay in college, the higher the probability they have of not completing their degree. The goal is to get them in and out of college as soon as possible.

PART TWO

LOWERING YOUR EXPECTED FAMILY CONTRIBUTION

7. WHAT IS FINANCIAL AID?

There are three types of financial aid: Need-based aid, Merit-based Aid, and Other financial aid.

Need - The need-based aid is your family income, your assets, and the number of people in college. The college is going to determine your financial aid based on a formula for your EFC (Expected Family Contribution).

EFC is derived from the financial aid forms that you will complete as part of the college process. To give you a rough number, take 20% of your income and 5.6% of your assets and add them together to determine the total EFC.

Income x 20% _____ + Assets x 5.6% _____ = EFC

Here's an example:

Adjusted Gross Income = $100,000

Multiply $100,000 by 20% = $20,000

Assets (liquid) = $100,000 ($80,000 in stocks and $20,000 in checking and savings)

Multiply $100,000 by 5.6% = $5,600

Add the totals: $20,000 + $5,600 = $25,600 EFC

This is a rough estimate of what your EFC will be for college financial aid. You may also go to www.finaid.org

and input your financial information into the system to determine your eligibility.

Need-based financial aid will definitely vary from school to school. This is based on the cost of attendance and the college's financial capacity to give money.

Here is the magic formula: **COA – EFC = NEED**

Cost of Attendance (COA) Minus
Expected Family Contribution (EFC) Equals NEED

Colleges are going to account for any outside resources such as scholarships or grandparent contribution and will make adjustments accordingly.

You may not have a **need** at your local state university because most limits at the state level are low, however, you may have a **need** at your higher-tier public university, or you may have a **great need** at your private school where you could get the most money.

Don't shy away from private schools because they actually have more money to allocate to families. Because they have more money to give, they could actually give larger scholarships and tuition discounts to entice you to come to their college. Many times attending a private college can be the same cost as going to state university. Now, that's a great bargain for your money. I ask families, "Do you want at least the option to consider a public or private college at the same cost?"

Merit - Merit aid is based on grades, GPA, class rank, SAT® scores, and co-curricular activities. I have seen merit aid as much as $30,000 a year at private colleges. The merit aid will vary based on a student's academic profile and the type of college that the student is applying. Most colleges will have a sliding scale based on GPA and SAT®

scores. The higher the scores and GPA the better award that they can receive. However, there are some colleges such as the Ivy colleges that do not award any merit aid. These colleges are 100% need-based financial aid. If you are not a need-based candidate at the Ivy Colleges, and get admitted, the cost of attendance will be the full price.

The Ivy Colleges are very generous if you have a **need**, and the majority of the time it will be **100% need met** to the family. This means that if the cost of attendance is $60,000 and your EFC is $20,000, then you will receive financial aid of $40,000 to attend that university.

Other Money - Other money is really how much money do you have in your bank account. The colleges are looking for any funds that can be used for college. Do you have any 529 plans? Do you have trust funds? Do the grandparents have college funds?

Here is my philosophy; the more you have in your liquid accounts the more you will have to pay for college. The assessment is a 5.6% of liquid assets that will be contributed to the Expected Family Contribution.

Let's take a closer look and add the component of *modified need* into the equation using an example of a private scholarship or *merit-based aid*.

Cost of Attendance Minus Expected Family Contribution Equals Need, Less Private Scholarship = *Modified Need*

Example:

COA $36,000 - EFC $16,000 = Need $20,000
Less $2000 Private Scholarship = Modified Need $18,000

In this example, you will be eligible for *need-based aid* of $20,000, but a $2000 scholarship *(merit)* was sent directly to the college. The college automatically deducts this amount from what you could have received.

If you have college accounts, some of the colleges may be blending the need and merit together.

Let's take another example using other money. If you had a 529 plan of $50,000, do you think you still have a need?

If you have a $50,000 529 plan and the cost of attendance at the college is $36,000; do you think the college is going to give you money?

The answer is NO!

You may still get some *merit* aid from a college regardless of your income. However, if you have a financial *need* and you have "college accounts" it will be very unlikely that you will receive any *need* based financial aid for the year.

You can still apply for financial aid next year, but the amount that you may receive could be much less. The colleges award majority of the money in the first year of college. This is because there is no longer any incentive to give you money. Your student is in their second year of college, has met new friends, and has made the adjustment into their new home. Do you really think the college is going to give you the maximum amount of money? They may still give some money, but it is very unlikely you will get the full amount after the first year.

Here's the bad part. If the student attends a college that considers their financial aid awards during the base year, then you will not get any money for the duration of the college years. The base year is the year that the student is entering college.

For example, if you did not get any money the first year at the university and the college is a "Base Year" financial aid assessment, you will not get a single penny from college to attend for the remaining years.

You want to maximize all of your money the first year entering into a college.

You are going to need to strategize and find colleges that are going to be best fitting to your case based on academics, and your financial capability.

8. FINANCIAL AID FORMS

What type of form is required for financial aid?

FAFSA – *Free Application for Federal Student Aid* – All colleges use the FAFSA form. This form is available for you on www.fafsa.ed.gov. You will also be able to view the form online and print out the FAFSA worksheet prior to filing your form. All of the forms are completed and submitted online. This form will determine your eligibility for financial aid and this includes any student/parent loans.

Some colleges make this as part of the whole entire process, if you do not want to complete a FAFSA because your income is too high, you are not obligated to file. However, some colleges will use this form as leverage for their benefit. They can entice you to send your student to their college by reviewing your financial data.

How can they use the FAFSA?

The FAFSA will show what other colleges your student has applied to, and what colleges you are considering. If you have applied to rival colleges, the colleges may use this information as an advantage. One college may really want to admit you, and may give you an offer to entice you to consider their campus instead of their competitor.

Common Mistakes on the FAFSA

- Name and Social Security Numbers do not match
- Dates of Birth are incorrect
- The student and parent information is switched
- If parents are divorced, only one parent information is required
- Retirement assets are not included
- Primary Home Equity is not required
- Completed the form late, past the deadline
- Completing the sign off at the end of the FAFA for submission

This form is pretty straight forward, and there are really only a few things that you need to be aware of when completing this form.

One is the question regarding your assets: Do not include your home equity or your retirement accounts in this question.

Secondly, if you are separated or divorced, your divorce decree or your separation agreement may be required. The college may want to verify if your ex-spouse has to pay a certain amount for college. The college may inquire whether or not there was a college fund set up in the separation process. All of this information may be verified.

CSS Profile Form - This is another financial aid form and or merit-aid form that private colleges will use to determine your eligibility for need-based aid or merit-based aid. Yes, merit-based aid, too.

I have to wonder why a college is going to ask about a family's income and assets for merit aid. I know this does not make any sense, but it's true.

This form is available on the **Collegeboard** website,

http://student.collegeboard.org/css-financial-aid-profile.

This form is very lengthy and can be very confusing for many families. I call this form the "Evil Form" because they really ask so many questions about your life. Some colleges have supplemental questions and are asking about the type of car you drive, the make, model, year, and how much you owe on the vehicle. They may also ask about your life insurance policy, and if you have any cash values in them. What do these questions have to do with your student's ability to get financial aid or merit aid? Nothing! It has nothing to do with it at all. The college is asking questions about your lifestyle and looking for any money that can be used for college.

9. ENROLLMENT MANAGEMENT

What is Enrollment Management? It's the selective use of offers of what colleges do to shape the incoming freshman class.

I'm going to give you the Wikipedia[1] version:

Enrollment Management is a term coined by Dr. Jack Maguire of Maguire Associates that is used frequently in higher education to describe well-planned strategies and tactics to shape the enrollment of an institution and meet established goals. Plainly stated, enrollment management is an organizational concept and a systematic set of activities designed to enable educational institutions to exert more influence over their student enrollments.[2]

Such practices often include marketing, admission policies, retention programs, and financial aid awarding. Strategies and tactics are informed by collection, analysis, and use of data to project successful outcomes. Activities that produce measurable improvements in yields are continued and/or expanded, while those activities that do not are discontinued or restructured.

Competitive efforts to recruit students are a common

---

[1] http://en.wikipedia.org/wiki/Enrollment_management#endnote_hossler

[2] Answers.com "Enrollment Management in Higher Education"

emphasis of enrollment managers.

The numbers of universities and colleges instituting offices of "Enrollment Management" have increased in recent years. These offices serve to provide direction and coordination of efforts of multiple offices such as admissions, financial aid, registration, and other student services. Often these offices are part of an enrollment management division.

Some of the typical aims of enrollment management include:

- Improving yields at inquiry, application, and enrollment stages.
- Increasing net revenue, usually by improving the proportion of entering students capable of paying most or all of unsubsidized tuition ("full-pays")
- Increasing demographic diversity
- Improving retention rates
- Increasing applicant pools

One example of an enrollment management platform is DecisionDesk, a web-based service that streamlines the submission and review process for hundred of colleges, universities, and various artistic and academic programs, festivals, and competitions across the world. The platform was created to help these institutions and ones like it to diversify and increase their applicant pools, to make the application process more accessible and easier for both long-distance and local applicants, and to streamline the way reviewers and administrators make their decisions.

According to Matthew Quirk[3] of The Atlantic Monthly,

---

[3] Matthew Quirk, 2005 The Best Class Money Can Buy, The Atlantic Monthly, Nov. 2005; Matthew Quirk, op. cit.

"More-advanced enrollment managers also tend to focus as much on retaining admitted students as on deciding whom to recruit and accept. They smooth out administrative hassles, guarantee at-risk students the advising and academic help they need, and ensure that the different parts of the university's bureaucracy work together to get students out the door with a degree."

This is the business side of college and how they operate. How does this apply to your student and family? The college will use your students GPA, Test Scores, FAFSA, and CSS Profile information and input this criteria into a system that will determine if your student will be a good fit for the college. It will also help the college decide how much need or merit aid to offer your student. The system will also provide some probability factors of your enrollment based on the award amount.

I find this process very intriguing, but this process is also very complicated. There are many factors that the college has to take into consideration when comprising the admissions pool, while being sensitive with the college's budget and goals.

If you have a sophomore or junior in high school, you most likely have been receiving plenty of mail from colleges? Have you been getting mail from colleges that you have never heard of before? Have you ever picked up the envelope and felt the quality of the paper and said, "Nice Paper! We should look into this college and check them out?" The mail begins to pour in right after your student takes the PSAT. The colleges obtained your student's scores and personal information to begin the marketing campaign. Have you noticed that the packets that you receive from the college are of high quality? The envelopes are textured and the letters seem to be personally signed by the college admissions director or counselor. The packets that they send you are very enticing and portray the college to be prestigious. It makes you want to go to their website and research the college immediately.

The colleges will be persistent and consistent with their marketing campaign. Does this mean that your student is going to automatically be admitted since the college is spending their resources in marketing to your family? The answer is NO, they are just marketing to you at this point in time to create awareness and to get your student to consider applying to their college.

Let me share with you a little bit more about this process, and what colleges can do or how they use the data that they receive from the testing organizations. The colleges will perform some data mining, statistical analysis, table analysis, and demographic checks. Here is what a college can do if they really wanted to find out more about a certain target market. The colleges can purchase lists from the public school system and get the students GPA and SAT scores. If your student is attending a private high school they cannot get this information, but they will do some reverse engineering to determine the GPA based on your students SAT/ACT scores. Once the college has the GPA, SAT/ACT scores they may take this a little further and look at your zip code. The college will see what the average income is in your neighborhood and see if the typical family in the neighborhood can afford to send their child to their college. If the really wanted to, the college will take a look at the past students that have applied to their college in the zip code, look at acceptance rates, look at the average awards of those students, and calculate the probability of your student attending their college based on these factors to see what made those student decide to commit. The college can gather most of information about your student before they even apply to the college.

This process is very similar to what banks have been doing to you by sending you pre-approved car loans or credit cards. Ever wonder how they got your name and address? How did they pre-approve you? They got your credit score somehow and started mailing to you. College is a business and one of their main goals is to fill seats, sequentially to maximize their revenue and minimize their expenses. The college will take the necessary actions and allocated resources in order to fulfill this goal.

PART THREE

FUNDING COLLEGE

10. SHOW ME THE MONEY

How do I fund college?

Every family has a unique case. I cannot give you financial advice at this point in time on how to fund your child's education. Although, I can tell you that most families will have up to six options to fund for college. The families may also use a combination of strategies to implement their college funding plan. You may want to contact me to discuss your personal case.

In this section, I want to give you a general sense of what you will be seeing on the financial aid awards and what the college will typically offer families.

There is always going to be some out-of-pocket cost for college expenses. There are 100% FREE rides, but these are rare cases with students amplifying extraordinary skills or talents. Majority of the time there are FREE Tuition Waivers or Grants and Scholarships that will cover the full amount of tuition. Essentially, the only expense to the family would be the food and housing. This cost will vary per college but the estimate is $12,000-$15,000.

What type of aid is available?

Grants - This is Free Money, no loans and no payback.

Here is a link to the federal grants for college

http://studentaid.ed.gov/

Here is the link for state grants in California
http://www.calgrants.org/index.cfm?navId=14

There are different types of grants that you will see on your financial aid awards: University Grant, Pell Grant, Cal Grant, and College Grant.

The federal and state grants that you receive are typically need-based awards and are renewable every year based on student academic and/or family income. Most of the Federal and State Grants are based on income range. You can check with your state on the qualifications for educational grants for college.

Cal Grants - In California, there's a **Cal Grant A** and a **Cal Grant B**. You still have to qualify for a **Cal Grant A**, and typically for a family of four, it's about $82,000 of adjusted gross income and under $60,000 of assets.

The Cal Grant Income Limits for California Families can be viewed at http://www.csac.ca.gov/doc.asp?id=916. Note that these limits of income and assets do change every year and you must qualify every year.

With a **Cal Grant A** you could receive up to $9,700 at a private university, up to $12,000 at a University of California (UC) college, and up to $5,500 at a California State University (CSU) for the year.

Additionally, California families with need may qualify for a **Cal Grant B**, and the student requirement is at least a 2.0 GPA.

For more information contact the California Student Aid Commission at http://www.csac.ca.gov/doc.asp?id=905. Note that the amounts of the State Grants may change every year so check your home state for the amount of the awards.

Pell Grants - Pell grants are income based, and typically for lower income families. This is federal money and the amounts do change every year.

Here is a link to their website so you can view your qualifications: http://www.csac.ca.gov/doc.asp?id=916

College and University Grants - These grants can be a combination of need-based and merit-based awards. These awards are typically renewable for four years on condition that the student is in good academic standing. The money is coming from the college, and in some cases, the college may want to simply "recruit" a particular student to attend so they may award that student a high award called a University Grant. It's considered financial aid, but it may be given to students who don't even qualify for financial aid.

Scholarships - The scholarships are merit awards and are typically renewable every year provided that the student maintains the required GPA. Consequently, the college will determine the minimum standard requirement to maintain the award. Typically, the higher the amount awarded, the higher the GPA requirement. Many colleges will have a sliding scale of merit-based aid awards on GPA and/or SAT scores. This type of award is given during the freshman year and is renewable every year. Some colleges will require the family to continue and complete the FAFSA in order to renew their scholarship award. You need to verify with the college's requirement on the renewal criteria.

Loans - There are a few different types of loans that will be available for students and parents. The federal loans will vary in amount per year for the student. This amount will range from $5,500 during the freshman year to $7,500 during senior year.

Federal Direct Loans Subsidized - This is a loan from the federal government. The interest and payments on this type of loan are deferred until six months after graduation.

Federal Direct Loans Un-Subsidized - This is a loan from the federal government and the interest is accruing while student is in college. You can begin making payments on this type of loan immediately, or defer the loan until six months after graduation.

Here is the link for more information on the Federal Direct Loans http://studentaid.ed.gov/types/loans/subsidized-unsubsidized

Federal Direct Parent Plus Loan - This is a loan from the federal government and one parent can sign on the loan and receive up to the full cost of attendance.

Here is the information for the parent plus loan http://www.direct.ed.gov/parent.html

Private Student Loan or Private Parent Loan - These loans are called "private" because the federal government does not fund them. This loan is typically done through a bank or credit union. The rates are typically lower and the term is twenty years. You need to verify the rate and term with the financial institution before obtaining the loan.

11. FREQUENTLY ASKED QUESTIONS

I have lots of home equity in my primary house, should I still apply for financial aid?

Yes, many colleges do not look at your primary residence home equity and do not count it in the EFC calculation. However, there are private colleges that use the CSS Profile form and they will consider your home equity in the EFC calculation. Here is something that you should understand, there are private colleges that only use the FAFSA and have large endowment funds. This means that you should consider applying to these types of colleges because the probability of getting more Free money is greater.

What if I make too much money to qualify for financial aid?

Remember that there is merit-based aid even if you make too much money. You have to know your EFC and if your EFC can be lowered to be under the cost of attendance, you can still receive need-based financial aid.

I have a 529 plan or other type of college fund. Will it hurt me?

Yes and No.

If you are from an affluent family with an income over $300,000 per year, a college account is acceptable for you. The reason is because your EFC is already high and, unfortunately in your case, you will never qualify to be a need-based candidate.

If you are a need-based candidate for private colleges with income under $300,000 per year, a college account may hurt you more than help you.

If your income is under $180,000 per year, a college account will most likely hurt your ability to get need-based aid at private colleges.

In some cases, the colleges will be blending your need and merit together. And having a college account will not be the wisest thing for your situation. You are going to want to do some strategic planning because you still can receive a good amount of free money for college.

Public Colleges will give need and merit awards and the income to qualify for need-based awards at many of the public colleges are under $80,000 AGI. You will have to verify the income range with the college because each state will have a different income limits. If you are planning to attend an out-of-state college, you will most likely be paying a higher fee because you are not a resident of the state. Again, there are certain programs such as the Western Undergraduate Exchange that may allow you to pay a lower fee if you qualify.

What if my grades are low, can I still get money for college?

Define low? The minimum I suggest is a 3.0 GPA. If your GPA is lower than this, you should consider a community college first and then transfer to a university in a few years.

You can still receive grants and scholarships with a 3.0 GPA, but do not expect a FREE RIDE. However, in California you may still qualify for a Cal Grant or Pell Grant if you meet the GPA and Income Criteria. If you are applying to private colleges and you have a low 3.0 GPA, you may still receive need-based awards such as university grants.

Do colleges compete for students?

Yes, colleges want good students with high GPA and Test Scores. Colleges offer large awards to these types of students. This is a way for the college to entice the student to attend their institution... with MONEY!

One strategy to use if you have the grades and the scores is to apply to like-like colleges that are attracting the same type of students of your caliber. The colleges will compete for you, and you may see that one college will offer a much higher award than the other college.

My high school does a college night and the counselor will go over all of the information, do I need additional help?

You don't know what you don't know. I'm sure you have great counselors at your school, but at some schools there are simply too many students and only a few counselors. Most of the counselors at public high schools are over worked and swamped with a workload of 200-300 students.

Most counselors will go over the general information on college admissions and financial aid. However, they will not cover strategies, financial planning, and/or positioning for college. The counselors will not go in depth about your financial case and does not discuss strategies to lower your EFC. The counselors are mainly going to go over the admissions aspect of college and do not help you with your college funding plans. They are going to be a great source of information on colleges and potential scholarships that you can consider.

I have a CPA and Financial Planner, they should be able to do complete the college financial aid forms for me, right?

I'm sure that they have seen the financial aid forms before, but most financial professionals are not up to date with the recent changes in the college financial aid system. If you speak to your accountant and ask about your net worth, they will give a figure. However, the net worth that the college asks on the financial aid forms is calculated differently.

12. THE APPEAL PROCESS

Is an appeal a negotiation?

I like to call appeals a subtle way to negotiate. You have to remember that we are dealing with educational institutions, and you need to value their service to your family.

Can I really appeal for more money?

Yes!

How do I appeal?

Very simple, you ask for more money. Each college university is different and most will have an appeal process. You may find the appeal process on the college's website, or you can contact the Financial Aid Office and inquire on how to initial an appeal for financial assistance or college admission.

Are there different types of appeal cases?

Yes. There are four types of appeal cases.

Need-Based Appeal - The college did not meet your expected need, and you cannot afford to pay your expected out-of-pocket expenses.

Merit-Based Appeal - When your student is coming into the college in the top ten percent of the incoming Freshmen Class. If you feel that your student is worthy of getting a higher merit award then what was given based on historic figures, you'll want to make an appeal.

Competitive Appeal - This kind of appeal works really well if you applied to rival colleges, and your student got into a rival college with more money. You simply ask to see if the other college can match the other award, or do a little better than the initial offer.

Special Circumstance Appeal - Perhaps there is a family member that has high medical expenses, or a grandparent that you are helping. The college does not see these expenses and you do not get to write these off on your tax return. You need to let the college know your case.

Are there appeals that do not work?

Yes. Here's a list of circumstances that may hinder an appeal.

- I have a high mortgage payment, and I can't pay for college. *That is a lifestyle choice.*
- I have other kids in private school. *May work at some colleges, but not at all colleges.*
- I have high credit card bills. *This would fall under lifestyle choice, as well.*
- I'm paying child support or alimony. *No, doesn't work either.*

13. PUTTING IT ALL TOGETHER: THE TIMELINE

Here is a timeline of activities that you should be creating and doing for the college bound student while in high school.

I've separated them in two categories: Junior year and Senior year.

Junior Year Activities

- Career search

- Aptitude testing

- PSAT®, if not done already

- SAT®/ACT test

- Begin college search

- Check status of high school path

- Begin work on resume

- Begin work on letters of recommendation

- Begin search for scholarships

- Start college visits

Senior Year Activities

- Finish strong academically
- SAT®/ACT again
- Refine college search
- More college visits
- September to November: Finalize these items
- Applications
- Resume
- Letters of recommendation
- Essays
- Scholarship forms
- November: Complete your profile
- December: Institutional forms
- January: FAFSA
- Housing applications
- March to April: Award letters arrive
- Award acceptance and response by May 1st

14. CASE STUDIES & STORIES

I'd like to share some of my client stories and case studies, and although their identities have been changed, the situations are true. My hope is that you may be able to better understand and relate to the process of college planning so that you may realize the success that can be attained when it's done properly.

First, you need to understand that there are some things to consider in the future of higher education with respect to the colleges: Their mission, ranking, competition for students, need for tuition revenue, diversity on campus, and graduation rates—the overall improvement of a student's persistence in graduating.

The previous items are a short and general detail of what each college considers, and what contributes to how they actually rank. Colleges are looking for all those different things (and more). The whole process of a college education, and the business of higher education have dramatically changed over the past twenty to thirty years—since the late 1980's—the biggest paradigm shift is the rise of enrollment management.

Enrollment management is the strategic use of offers of which colleges make to shape the composition of the incoming freshmen class in furtherance of the institutional goals. It is to be distinguished from the allocation of financial aid based on the student's need or academic merit. "Manny, what does that mean?" Basically, it's the science of how colleges are going to recruit and allocate financial aid.

This is now a standard practice at all private universities and most public schools. Every college has adopted this application. It's not what you need. It's what the college needs.

So here is a perspective of the college or enrollment management as an example: "If we need a minority student, we will recruit one. We will get a minority student by offering more grants or university grants for the family to come to our college."

Here are some other examples of what the college needs or wants. If the college wants more females majoring in Engineering, then they will find them and recruit them. If the college is in New York State and wants a student from California because they want to diversify the university, then they will pay to get a student from California to come to that college.

This is the business side of college and enrollment management.

Consider some questions. Do you have a senior student in high school that is getting a lot of mail from a wide variety of colleges? Or, has your junior student recently scored well on the PSAT®, and you are now getting mail from colleges across the nation? The colleges actually bought the list from College Board. The college narrowed a search and said, "I want kids in this GPA and this SAT® score range. I'm going to mail to these families and these students could possibly qualify to come to my college." It's smart target marketing! So again, it's not what you need. It is what the college needs.

Now, let's look at some of those case studies of families that I have worked with, and the kind of money they received.

Case #1 – Lower Income Family

Ken from Tracy High

4.2 GPA

1380 Critical Reading and Math score

2020 Total SAT®

Family income $52,000

$30,000 in liquid assets

$400,000 in equity and rentals

$100,000 in home equity

EFC at the time is $32,800, and based on the EFC, the college believes that he can pay $30,000 a year with $52,000 of income. It doesn't make sense, right? Well, it does. But, here's what happened.

Ken's Result:

Accepted into the University of San Diego

Awarded $33,000

Student loans of $7,000 (reimbursed)

Ken has to pay back the student loans. Essentially, he's going to this college for less than the cost of going to a community college. We get a large portion of money because the student had an impressive GPA and he had a fairly good SAT® score.

Case #2 - Middle Income Family:

Jennifer from Valley Christian High School

Biology, pre-med

1450 Critical Reading and Math score

Total SAT® 2190

Initial pick for college is one, and then we applied to nine colleges

$110,000 income

Taxable investment $150,000

$150,000 in home equity

We have four members in the family with one in college

Initial EFC is $30,400 and we were able to reduce the final EFC to $29,000

Jennifer's Result:

Accepted into UNC Chapel Hill.

Awarded a scholarship of $15,000.

We got a Stafford Loan that needs to be repaid, so the cost of savings at this time is $27,398, but we're going to an   out-of-state Tier 1 college for $9,770 per year—out-of-pocket.

The total savings for college over four years is $70,500.

Awesome! Man, this kid's Dad is fired up. He loves me. His daughter is going to attend UNC Chapel Hill for less than $10,000 a year.

Let's take a look at this case closer. You see, the college said the EFC is $30,400. We are really paying only $10,000; our EFC doesn't really matter anymore in this case.

Case #3 – High Income Family:

Alice from Fremont High School

Communications, public relations and business major

SAT® 1360 / 1980

3.85 GPA

Considering 15 colleges nationwide and then applied to 7

Family income $139,000

Taxable investments $190,000

An estate coming worth $150,000

$180,000 in home equity

We have four members in the family with two in college (1st student at Cornell and parents are paying $52,779 per year)

Initial EFC is $28,520 and we were able to reduce the final EFC to $13,900

Alice's Result:

Accepted Villanova University in Pennsylvania.

Cost of Attendance (COA): $48,270 per year

Received: $20,000 Villanova Grant

$5,500 Subsidized Loan

$7,500 Villanova-Loan

$33,400 Total Aid

Out-of-pocket for parents is now just $15,270 per year

Case #4 – High EFC / High Income Family:

Nancy from Cal High

4.3 GPA

ACT 33 / 36

Family income $265,000

Non-Retirement Assets & Mutual Funds $185,000

Stocks $87,000

529 Plans for all 4 kids $125,000

$486,000 in home equity

Initial EFC is $119,100 and we were able to reduce the final EFC to $59,500

Nancy's Result:

Accepted into 8/10 colleges

Private schools offered $15,000-$20,000 in grants per year

Nancy chose Santa Clara University

Cost of Attendance (COA): $53,000 per year

Received: $30,500 SCU Grant

                     $7,000 Trustee Scholarship

                     $37,500 Total Award = FREE MONEY

Out-of-pocket for parents is now just $15,000 per year

Nancy is attending a private college for less than a state university!

You see, this family called me after seeing my interview featured in Money Magazine. After they read the article they call me and said, "Hey, I saw you in this magazine. Can you help me?"

I said, "Sure, I could help you but you're not a financial aid candidate."

And he said, "Well, how can you help me if I'm not a financial aid candidate?"

I said, "It's all about how you position your student for college and how you position your finances for college."

Here's the result and I'll reiterate what happened here. We did some financial planning and some positioning. We reduced our EFC by 50% from $119,100 to $59,500, and we got accepted into 8/10 colleges. One of the 10 colleges was Cal Poly San Louis Obispo. His daughter wanted to major in Engineering, and if you know about Cal Poly, it's a national ranking college for Engineering.

The disadvantage about Cal Poly, SLO is that the college wants the student to declare their major and does not allow them to change.

Do you remember what it was like being a seventeen year old? Most 17-year-old young adults have no clue of what they want to do at that stage in life. The odds are that the student will change their mind.

In the end she decided to go to Santa Clara University. It's a great regional school that has a national ranking. It also has a great engineering program that Apple and other Silicon Valley companies recruit from.

When you think about it the out-of-pocket cost is equivalent to the housing, and the out-of-pocket cost is just $15,000 per year. Attending Santa Clara University is now less than it would cost than to going to a state university.

Case #5 – High EFC Family:

Chris from a Bellarmine College Preparatory

Liberal Arts Major – Desiring law school

3.78 GPA

Critical Reading & Math 1320

SAT® 2020

Considering 7 colleges nationwide

Family income $134,000

$10,000 in taxable assets (liquid)

Initial / Final EFC $34,000 per year

Chris's Story and Results: Chris, a student from a private high school in the area, and his family that didn't have much money other than the $10,000 in liquid savings, had an EFC of $34,000 per year. We set out to apply for colleges and Chris got accepted into Hiram, Wooster, and Oberlin in Ohio. All of these colleges are looking for the same type of student.

Here are some award offers before I continue the story.

- Hiram University COA is $36,380 and Chris received an initial award of $5,000 per year.
- Wooster University COA is $39,305 and Chris received an initial award letter of $15,000 per year.
- FAFSA submitted – updated award letter of a half-tuition waiver, $15,000 per year and an opportunity to earn the other half from scholarship competition.

The student was offered to come to a scholarship interview, and our strategy was more or less a competitive appeal.

We ended up getting a **free ride to Hiram** because we showed them all the offers from Wooster and Hiram said, "Look, we want you to come here." Chris knocked the ball out of the park in the interview, and they absolutely loved this kid. They said, "If you want to come to our college, we'll offer you a free ride here, so let us know. Here's our offer."

And the family calls me up and says, "Manny, we got the free ride. Should we take it?"

I respond, "Why are you asking me, take the money Chris. You got a free ride, go for it! You don't need to call me to take the free ride. Take it! Where is your mom at?"

"She's right here, Manny. She told me to call you."

I said, "Hey, no problem and congratulations. Take the money and I'll see you when you get back home."

Sometimes, it will work out in your favor if you go back for the scholarship interviews. The bottom line in this particular case, it was an increase of $31,380 from the initial offer of just $5,000, and ultimately a FREE TUITION RIDE totaling $145,520 in FREE MONEY for college.

Case #6 – High EFC & High Income (Affluent) Family:

Alex – St. Francis High School

4.1 GPA

SAT® 2280

Income $1,639,000 (Bay Area CEO)

Non-Retirement Assets $1,700,00 (1.7 million)

Retirement Accounts $4,500,000 (4.5 million)

529 Plan

$5,000,000 in home equity & real estate holdings

Yes, five million dollars

EFC ... WAY TOO HIGH!

Let me tell you a story about this family. A woman attends one of my free college planning workshops in San Jose, California and then schedules an appointment to come into the office.

She brings with her all of the information for me to review regarding their case as shown above.

I immediately look at the woman and ask, "How can I help you, and what are you looking for today?"

She replies with, "We do not want to pay full price for college, and we would like to know how to pay less."

I looked at her with a smile and told her, "I'm sorry, but I think you wasted your time today. You have income and assets to pay for college and there is not much I can help you with here. I see that you can set up your own scholarship fund to help other students."

She replies with, "I was referred to you by other executive families that worked with you."

She proceeded to say, "you have saved them money during this process and I would like to save some money too."

I continue the conversation and ask, "What does your husband have to say about this process?"

She says, "That's not my husband, that's my employer." She went on to explain that she handles all of his personal affairs.

I explained that I couldn't talk to her about this matter until I speak with her employer and asked, "Can you get him on the phone with me?" She agrees and a few moments later I'm discussing the matter with this executive. I go through my quick evaluation and ask him what his criteria for college is for his son.

He tells me that he does not want to pay $60,000 for college and does not want his son to attend a UC College. He wants a college with a little bit of "panache."

Alex's Result:

Accepted into Cornell, Duke, UCB, UCSC and Amherst College, MA

Awarded $18,500 Amherst Grant

Only offer was Amherst, no other college offered money

Cost of Attendance (COA) at Amherst: $58,000 per year

Out-of-pocket for the executive is $39,500 per year

We got $18,500 off tuition at Amherst!

So the father calls me and asks, "How did we get money?"

I told him, "You just got bought! The college sees you as part of their future endowment fund."

I continue to explain, "The college is giving you a discount because they may want you donate money to their school in the future. Does this make sense? Absolutely! They (the college) give you about $80,000 of FREE money over four years. They gamble that you will give hundreds of thousands, if not millions in the future. They are going to have the bragging rights to mention that the Bay Area-Silicon Valley CEO's are sending their kids to Amherst. You get to tell all of your friends at the country club that you are getting a discount at Amherst. It's a fair trade!"

I say to him, "Are you in or out?"

He says, "We're in!"

I said, "Great! Write your check and you're done. Don't forget to tell all of your friends about me."

Awards and Admission News:

Although the list of awards and admissions is constantly growing, I'd like to share with you some good news with some families I work with.

You can stay current on our awards, admissions and college planning news by liking us on Facebook, https://www.facebook.com/collegeplanningabc

Here's how we celebrate with some recent posts...

Congrats Phil, he got a $12,000/year scholarship offer from Colorado School of Mines (essentially bringing cost down to in-state tuition), plus a full-tuition offer letter from Chadron State U.

Admissions to U of Arizona, ASU, San Diego State, University of Portland with $17,000 off!

USD with $25,000, ASU with $15,000, University of Nevada, Reno with $15,500 off, and Another USF with $20,000 per year, UCR admissions, St. Mary's with $11,000/year

USF admission with $20,000 per year and University of Illinois, Urbana, Champaign Admission for Engineering!

More Great News - What an Awesome Day!
SCU - $21K/ Yr ($84,000 off 4 yrs)
USF - $20K/ yr ($80,000 off 4 yrs)
LMU - $13K/ Yr ($52,000 off 4 yrs)
Chapman - $20K/ yr ($80,000 off 4 yrs)

Over 75 more admissions from this morning... 5 USC, 4 UCLA, 9 UCSD, 7 UCSC, 15 UCD, 22 SCU, 11 CalPoly, 3 Rensselaer (RPI), 2 RoseHulman

Money-Money-Money! SCU $21,000 - USF $20,000 LMU $13,000 - Chapman $20,000 - Redlands $18,500

Another huge award from USF $43,000 x 4 yrs = $172,000

USF Admissions with $176,000 over 4 years! This is the highest award so far at USF for my students.

Admissions to LMU with $18,500/ yr ($74,000 off over 4 yrs)

Admissions to Northeastern with $22,500/yr ($90,000 over 4 yrs)

Admissions to Santa Clara University with $27,800/ yr ($111,2000 over 4 yrs)

UCSD, UCI, UCSB, UCD and another Boston University

Admissions to University of San Diego with $25,000 per year (100K off College), and an invite to honors program.

Admissions to UC Riverside with $2000 per year with Honors Program!

Admissions to Skidmore, SCU, Villanova, Northeastern, USF, Ithaca!!

Admitted UoP (5 year dental program), Santa Clara, UC Davis, UCSD

Boston University 7 yr Medical School acceptance with $15,000 per year!

$40,000/ $60,000/ $74,800 off 4 yrs... I love this time of year!

$208,000 off Claremont McKenna for 4 years!!! Yeah Baby!!!

Your award news could be posted next so connect with us at https://www.facebook.com/collegeplanningabc

15. How To Really Get Free Money For College

Positioning Yourself and Your Student Properly To Maximize Financial Aid Opportunities

Let me keep it simple with three points.

- Academic planning
- Student positioning into the right colleges
- Parent financial positioning

If you do these three things you will be in good shape to save some BIG MONEY!

There is a lot of information that we have covered together throughout this process. We talked about standardized testing, selecting the right colleges, what colleges want, and how you should apply for financial aid. I presented the myths and dispelled the myths; especially the one that says financial aid is not available to those with assets and a decent income. It's simply not true. Free money for college is available regardless of your assets or your income!

There are a few things I want you to understand.

First, I want you to understand positioning. There are two

kinds: one is student positioning and the other is parent positioning.

Second, I want you to understand positioning properly. Regardless of your income and your assets, that if you know how to apply to the right colleges, you could still get financial aid or merit-based aid for your student—as long as you are applying to the right colleges.

Third, you also need to understand cash flow, and how to pay for college, because—no matter what—you're going to have to pay some out-of-pocket costs.

Ultimately, the question becomes how do you fund college without sacrificing your lifestyle and your retirement at the same time? I can help.

So what's next?

If you want to take advantage of a free thirty-minute consultation with me either on the telephone or in my office, I'd love to have you on my calendar.

If you want to get some expert advice and figure out how to save some time and save your stress level, I can help you navigate through this college planning maze.

Please visit us online http://www.collegeplanningabc.com or call our office at 408-918-3068 to set up your consultation with one of my friendly staff members.

Simply tell my staff the secret booking code...

"I read Manny's book!"

You'll receive a FREE thirty-minute consultation (valued at $297.00). I appreciate you, and hope you found this book to be a valuable time-saver as well as resourceful. I look forward to seeing you or speaking with you, and I wish you all the best in your college planning process.

GLOSSARY OF TERMS
(THAT COLLEGES DO NOT WANT YOU TO KNOW)

&

OTHER RESOURCES

Glossary Of Terms
That Colleges Do Not Want You To Know

Admit-Deny: The process of ranking students who have already been accepted to the college. i.e. A college wants 500 freshmen, it sends 1500 acceptance letters, uses aid to entice the 500 most wanted students.

Application Score: A scoring system used (in differing formats) by every college. It's how they rank their applicants. Some colleges use a number system or letter system to sort. Most colleges will have an applicant's package read by two admissions officers. If your student's score is above the cutoff mark, they admit; below, they reject; and between the two marks, a committee decides your student's fate.

Flag: A student's record has been marked for special consideration. i.e. Children of alumni may get a flag, or students with special talents, under-represented minorities. These applications usually are separated from the common pool and considered separately.

Financial-Aid Leveraging: Practice of cutting the sticker price to specifically targeted groups of applicants. The goal is to maximize the financial aid dollar and admit larger numbers of students with the same dollars. Or, the school may artificially depress the amount of aid given in a given year, to see if that level of aid can become the new "baseline."

Gender-balance: Some universities require a student body to be comprised of certain ratios of men-to-women. Admissions and financial aid offices then attempt to build a class with these pre-determined characteristics.

Preferential Packaging: Polite term for buying freshmen. 54 percent of colleges admit to following this practice.

Buying Freshmen: The students who are most attractive to a college get the best financial aid package, or more grants and free money and less loans and work-study. Can also take the form of large tuition discounts, or giving more aid than the student's need.

Legacy Rating: Children of Alumni are called legacies, and sometimes have an advantage over others in the admissions process (not true in the financial aid process). The size of the admissions advantage may be determined by the parent's generosity in alumni fund drives.

RESOURCES & SCHOLARSHIP WEBSITES

- www.collegeboard.com
- www.collegeprowler.com
- www.collegetoolkit.com
- www.fastweb.com
- www.finaid.com
- www.scholarships.com
- www.scholarships4students.com
- www.zinch.com

COLLEGE PLANNING ABC

College Planning ABC is the premier college planning company in the Bay Area of California. Our goal is to match students with the right college—their dream school—and help parents find the money to pay for it!

We use the following 16-point quality checklist guaranteed to recap and save you the most money on your college tuition costs:

- Assist you with your college search
- Conduct a thorough student interview
- Calculate your Expected Family Contribution (EFC)
- When applicable, make recommendations to reduce your EFC
- Make recommendations to pay for your EFC on a tax-favored basis
- Complete the Federal Student Aid (FAFSA) application
- Register for the College Scholarship Service (CSS) Profile
- Complete the CSS Profile
- Confirm the accuracy of the Student Aid Report (SAR), and make necessary adjustments
- Assist with verification forms
- Assist with any institutional forms
- Direct all financial aid negotiations
- Assist with Subsidized Stafford Loan application form
- Assist with Unsubsidized Stafford Loan application form
- Provide a "College Planning Checklist" of what will be done for you, and when it will be done
- Implement financial recommendations

Here are the types of families that we work with. The categories are separated into income levels. Where do you fit in?

Affluent ($250,000+) - Many affluent families seek help to get admitted to the best colleges in the nation, any discounts for them would be beneficial either in tuition discounts, tax deductions, saving time and less stress.

Upper Middle Income ($150,000-$250,000) - These families also need help because there is no "need- based" financial aid and no federal tax benefits. They can pay for college but would have to utilize all (or the majority) of their resources to pay for college.

Middle Income ($70,0000-$150,000) - Families want to get their child to the top colleges and get discounts to make it affordable. These families make too much money to qualify for certain types of financial aid, and don't have all of the money to fund college. These types of families need the most help. Working with our team will provide the resources on how to reduce the cost of college in grants, scholarships and providing solutions to pay for college.

Lower Income (Below $70,000) - Families want the best admissions and the best financial aid packages. They have a total financial need and want their child to go to some of the best colleges with little or no out of pocket cost to the family.

Other Families - Some families just want to get their child admitted to a college and attend. Their child is an average student and does not want to start off college at the local community college. Their student can qualify to be admitted to a university and are willing to send their child off to college somewhere.

The "I Just Want Some Help" Families - These families just have no time, and no patience to get their student to do anything. Usually, the student doesn't listen to the parent much at this age and parents just want someone else to help them through this process. This family is just tired and frustrated with their talented student that just won't listen to them. Parents, it's not your fault. It's hormonal! Give it a few more years, and they will come around more to talk to you. Give them ten years and then they will tell you, "I should have listened to you."

This is why when I meet or speak with you in our private one-on-one consultation, I inform the family if they are a good fit for me to work with, and if you can benefit from our relationship.

Here's what some of our clients have to say about College Planning ABC and working with Manuel Fabriquer.

Sylvia Roy writes:

I did not hesitate to attend the first seminar given by Manny when I received the flyer in the mail because we don't have any idea on how to start the college application process. Our son is the first in the family. I am glad I made the decision. Manny and his team helped us from the beginning to the end. Our son got accepted to different schools. He decided to go to a private school. After 3 financial aid denials, Manny again came in and at the end our son was awarded a total of $16,000 worth of scholarship and grants. Whew! This was a big financial relief for us. We couldn't have afforded the hundreds of thousands of school fees. We couldn't thank Manny enough for all the help.

God Bless, The Roy Family

Lynne Yamaichi writes:

Having three children within 18 months (oldest daughter then twin daughters) has been a hectic and fun ride! As they grew, college costs has been on our minds, and getting some advise here and there on how to save was what we were banking on.

In reality, with pre-college saving advice that was not in our best interest, the rise in college costs, and a 25% reduction in work for one parent, we were in trouble! Thank goodness with a referral from a friend, we met Manny! His college financial planning has set our family up so that we can see exactly how we are going to tackle this important milestone in our daughter's lives.

Manny has made it manageable and reassuring.

We have mixed emotions on having our two younger daughters leave for college, but at least financially, we are set, and most importantly, finances did not deter our daughters from choosing the university of their choice!

We appreciate ALL that Manny and College Planning ABC has done for our family!

Amy Yoshida from Milpitas, California writes:

If you have a student in high school that is planning on going to college, Manuel Fabriquer of College Planning ABC is the man for you! Not only does he guide you through the entire selection and application process, his knowledge and skill in getting you incredible financial aid is invaluable. He helped us get an amazing financial aid award, which basically paid full tuition for all four years at USC! Manny helped us find the perfect fit and the funds to get there, and for that we are forever grateful.

MEET THE AUTHOR

MANUEL FABRIQUER, CCPS

Certified College Planning Specialist
Founder & President of College Planning ABC

http://CollegePlanningABC.com

Manuel Fabriquer is the Founder and President of College Planning ABC in San Jose, California. He is a Certified College Planning Specialist and is recognized as a leading authority on the topic of college planning and your finances as seen in the Wall Street Journal, MSN Money, US News & World Report, FOX News and CNN, and has frequent appearances on a variety of national TV and radio programs.

Manny's thoughts on working with clients are simply stated by him personally: "I inform families if they are a good fit for me to work with and if you can benefit from our relationship. I only take on families that I know I can help save money or I know that I can meet their expectation. I only want to work with families that I can make the biggest impact. This is why my reputation in the industry has been impeccable and the public has responded in overwhelming response with hundreds of families coming through my Free College Planning Workshops every month."

If you would like to join us for one of our workshops, please visit us online to view our upcoming schedule at http://www.collegeplanningabc.com/free-workshops/

You can connect with College Planning ABC on facebook at https://www.facebook.com/collegeplanningabc or visit the company website at http://CollegePlanningABC.com.

College Planning ABC
560 S. Winchester Blvd # 500
San Jose, CA 95128
Phone: (408) 918-3068   Fax: (888) 276-8023
www.collegeplanningabc.com

Made in the USA
San Bernardino, CA
05 March 2016